To Melinda,
A truly Beautiful
Woman

With Love,

Linda Lapointe
6/28/07

Beautiful Women

Beautiful Women

Like You and Me

Photographer **Linda Lapointe**
Writer **Patty Mayeux**

Formatting and cover design by Anne McLaughlin, Blue Lake Design, Dickinson, Texas
Published in the United States by Baxter Press, Friendswood, Texas

ISBN: 978-1-888237-69-6

Printed in China

To all women,

especially those who have not yet recognized their own inner beauty.

Table of Contents

9   Acknowledgements

11   Introduction

13   *Broaden Your Base of Beauty*

14   Martha Beaver, Houston, TX
Peace

16   Monique Jean, Montréal, QC
Reverence

18   Rosa Davis, Anywhere, USA
Free Spirit

20   *Voices/Voces,*
Candy Torres

21   *Skin Deep,*
Mary Laufer

22   Robin Lyon, Sonoma, CA
Animal Attraction

24   Josée Simbabawe, Montréal, QC
Freedom

26   Lesley Parrott, Toronto, ON
Victor

28   tomiko Lalonde, Calgary, AB
Enlightenment

30   Joan Cobb-Beaumont,
Calgary, AB
Nature's Child

32   Isabella Fu, Seattle, WA
Success

34   Karin Meng, Los Altos Hills, CA
Advocacy

36   *She May Be Found,*
Nancy Gustafson

37   *The House Dress,*
Sue Mayfield-Geiger

38   Edna Shinn, Pasadena, TX
Independence

40   Nellie Chappell-White,
League City, TX
Communicator

42   Ketra Oberlander,
Santa Clara, CA
Artistic Vision

44   El March, Toronto, ON
Healer

46   Elizabeth Treviño, Sweeny, TX
Hope

48   Hellen Carreras, Seattle, WA
Square Peg

50   *Training Day,*
Lisa E. Beatman

52   Sarah Byam, Seattle, WA
Mental Health

54   Huguette Vervroegen,
S.-J. du Lac, QC
Earth Mother

56   Denyse Deschênes,
Wellington, NS
Bravery

58   Lisa McCleod, Snellville, GA
Imperfection

60   Yaffa Tsadyk, Forest Hills, NY
Overlooked Beauty

62   Gabriele Hilberg,
Mountain View, CA
Meditation

64   Carolina Loren,
Mississaugua, ON
Identity

66   *Black Women, Tired,*
Rolanda Pyle

67   *Pretty,*
Marion Deutsche Cohen

68   Gail Evans, Atlanta, GA
Intentional Life

70   Camelia Ades, Seattle, WA
Freedom to Choose

72   Sophie Canuel, Longueuil, QC
Serenity

74   Sharron Ragan, Marietta, GA
Integrity

76   Clea Kore, Corralitos, CA
Reciprocity

78   Helene Hines, Long Island, NY
Perseverance

80   *song for Johanna,*
Adele Graf

81   *The Road Near Two Gray Hills,*
David Feela

82   Ruby Cone, League City, TX
Native American Beauty

84   Beth Diehl, Kemah, TX
Tropical Beauty

86   Aleksandra Vander-Hoek,
Calgary, AB
Warmth

88   Gwen Faye, Duluth, GA
Fast Talent

90   *Imperfect Beauty,*
Danielle Ackley-McPhail

91   *I am not, I am,*
Shirley A. Jones

92   Iris Grimm, Atlanta, GA
Delayed Dreams

94   Camelia Espahbod, Seattle, WA
International Scholar

96   Nathalie Geddry,
Portuguese Cove, NS
Soul Music

98   Allison Husband, Calgary, AB
Balance

100   *The Women Behind Me,*
Anja Leigh

101   *Prayer for a Day,*
Jill Williams

102   Maile Roundtree, Kirkland, WA
Commitment

104   Yolanta Szule, Astonia, NY
Explorer

106   Devon Webster, Seattle, WA
Conqueror

108   Linda Lapointe

109   Patty Mayeux

111   Ordering information

Acknowledgements

We wish to thank the following for their encouragement and support of this project. For all those who believed in our purpose, understood our message and participated in or referred women for interviews: Camelia Ades, Bob Allgeier, Margee Anderson, Martha Beaver, Lindsey Benoit, Marsha Boetzer, Merlyn Brown, Judith Bruni, Sarah Byam, Sophie Canuel, Hellen Carreras, Judy Chambers, Stacey Chambers, Theresa Chan, Robert Chapman, Nellie Chappell-White, Elda Cisneros, Joan Cobb-Beaumont, Ruby Cone, Mandy Corley, Rosa Davis, Denyse Deschênes, Beth Diehl, Bonnie Drew, Gwen Faye Edwards, Sara Elward, Camelia Espahbod, Gail Evans, Janet Ferguson, Isabella Fu, Edouard Françisque, Nathalie Geddry, Gail Glasser, Jen Graham, Iris Grimm, Janet Griffith, Jim Guidry, Lynda Guidry, Isabelle Guinois, Linda Halpayne, Beth Hetrick, Dr. Gabriele Hilberg, June Hills, Helene Hines, Allison Husband, Marc Isaacs, Renee Jacoby, Emily Jean, Monique Jean, Marsha Johansen, Ashley Kircher, Andrew Konstantaras, Clea Kore, tomiko Lalonde, Patricia Lapointe, Pauline Lapointe, Kate Lind, Lis Lister, Carolina Loren, Robin Lyon, El March, Sue Mayfield-Geiger, Lisa McLeod, Dr. Karin Meng, Barbara Merino, Yvette Michaud, Carl Miller, Joan Neubauer, Ketra Oberlander, Melannie O'Connor, Karen Page, Lesley Parrott, Kristina Pelkey, Laura Pennino, Denise Perreault, Martha Phipps, Sharron Ragan, Suzanne and Sami Rassy, Mary Riggi, Charly Rok, Hardy Roper, Bonnie Ross-Parker, Maile Roundtree, Beth Schoenfeldt, Nancy Seifert, Edna Shinn, Josée Simbabawe, Toby Singhania, Carolyn Slette, Ava Sloan, Yolanta Szule, Lori Thomas, Beth Thrift, Brian Todd, Elizabeth Trevino, Barbara Trudeau, Yaffa Tsadyk, Aleksandra Vander-Hoek, Huguette Vervroegen, Betty Watson-Borg, Devon Webster and Wendy Woynillowicz.

For those who graciously supplied a place for us to stay during our travels: Marc Beaumont and Joan Cobb-Beaumont, Shelly and J. D. Goff, Patricia Lapointe and Christian Cusson, Lis and Bob Lister, Robin and Robert Lyon, Kristina Pelkey, and Maile and Brian Roundtree.

To Pat Springle of Baxter Press for publishing and printing advice.

For editing: Lynda Guidry, Duncan Hasell, Jessica Mayeux, Peggy Rhoades and Katherine Swarts.

For encouragement and advice when it was most needed: Elda Cisneros, Jim Guidry, Lynda Guidry, Olayinka Joseph, Jessica Mayeux, Rebecca Mayeux, Peggy Rhoads and Dorothy Waldman.

For all the poets who submitted their wonderful and heartfelt works and for everyone who supported us through words of affirmation and gentle suggestions throughout the project, you are too numerous to mention but our appreciation is deep.

And finally, to our spouses for unwavering support and encouragement throughout: Drew Bell and Steve Mayeux.

Introduction

Beautiful Women — Like You and Me is based on the notion that our society has defined beauty in narrow terms of an ideal physical appearance that few women can achieve. Linda and I believe all women will benefit from a broader definition that includes inner strength, determination, humor, generosity and love. Our aim is to inspire women to value their own inner beauty above that which is defined by physical beauty alone. We hope that all readers, women and men, will gain a new sense of admiration, respect and awe for the women they know.

Linda had three main factors to consider while photographing the women. The first was regarding the lighting conditions at each location. She preferred natural light, but on occasion, the use of flash was necessary. Next, Linda had to decide which elements to include in the photograph that would best depict something of the inner character of the woman. As I conducted the interviews, typically in the homes or work environments familiar to the women, Linda gained insight needed to help her create the best setting for the photograph. Finally, she was careful to preserve the reality of the women and kept photo retouching to a minimum.

Some women carefully selected what to wear and some were more casual, even wearing little or no makeup. We did not request that they prepare in any way, only to be themselves, and to be comfortable. The result is a collection of photographs depicting women who are truly beautiful in each occasion.

I have always enjoyed the interviewing aspect of journalism. My experience meeting the women featured in this book is a highlight of my writing career. My biggest challenge was to choose the one main theme for each of the short biographies. I frequently began with pages of typed notes for each woman and then began the long process of editing draft after draft. Much like a film editor, I had to leave a lot of good material on the cutting floor.

We spent a lot of time learning about the publishing industry and exploring our options. Patrick Springle was recommended and after meeting with him, we were excited to pursue publishing with Baxter Press.

We have truly enjoyed working together. Our shared sense of adventure made it easy for us to pick up and fly to any city that promised a few women for us to interview and photograph. We traveled to the following cities and surrounding areas: Atlanta, Calgary, Halifax, Houston, Montreal, New York, San Francisco, Seattle and Toronto. We met women who comprised a wide variety of nationalities, faiths, ages, ethnicities and abilities. That was the fun part. Unfortunately, not every woman could be included and we made some very tough decisions regarding which forty would make the final cut. We hope all the women we have met throughout our experience with this book know how wonderful, and beautiful, they really are.

Broaden Your Base of Beauty

PATTY MAYEUX

Barbie Doll Beauty
Has no place here.

Pale hair
Pale skin

Perky breasts
Little boy hips

Belong in
A plastic world

Created by man
And his ideals.

Seek the beauty within;
Be bold and let it shine.

Madison Avenue lies
With abnormal images.

The very thing
You hate the most

May be your own
Brand of beauty.

Eyes set deep in thought;
Round face, full of gentleness;
Dark, historic tones;
Regal angles hinting at nobility.

Embrace Beauty!
Not from without

But from within
And smile when you encounter it.

Peace

MARTHA BEAVER is finally at peace with the person she has become.

She has won several gold medals in the Senior World Games and is proud of her natural abilities. But it wasn't always so. Throughout childhood, Martha struggled with an unrealistic ideal her adoptive mother placed on her.

In high school Martha won awards for "boyish" games like powder puff football, but her mother, hoping Martha's athletic ability would turn to more feminine interests, encouraged her to take ballet. In her thirties, Martha received a package of memorabilia from her mother, containing only ballet shoes and dance costumes. The awards and trophies Martha had earned for less-than-feminine pursuits had been thrown out.

Martha has always loved to swim. Her favorite childhood memory is of freely floating off the shores of Lake Erie. She later coached swimming for ten years before moving to the Houston area. Recently, she began competitive swimming; her expectations were surpassed when she set personal records. At the Texas Senior Olympics she won three silver and two gold medals, and she went on to set three world records in the fifty-five- to fifty-nine-year-old division of the Senior World Games. Martha spends her free time bird watching, scuba diving, and volunteering on the tall ship *Elissa* in Galveston. Quiet moments spent on the deck of her waterfront home—watching a hummingbird hovering over a potted plant, a storm coming across the water, or a sailing ship gliding by—give her a radiant peace within. "Water ties you to God," Martha says. "Water has always given me peace."

As she has matured, she has come to recognize that true beauty is internal, rather than external. She admits it is a continuing struggle as she strives to reach that ideal. "The person who is constantly worried about everything never calms down long enough to find inner beauty," Martha says. "It's a constant grow."

Reverence

MONIQUE JEAN is passionate about serving others through prayer and song.

Her daily presence at her church in Montreal has earned her a reputation many would find hard to live up to, but Monique takes it all in stride. She finds joy singing in the choir, peace in worshipping daily, and, most of all, strength in praying for others. Monique receives many prayer requests. She is happy to give her time to prayer and surprised that she sometimes receives money for her intercession.

"I am blessed to have so many friends," Monique says. "I'm like a queen. It always makes me feel good."

Going to church reminds her of her childhood home in Haiti; she finds comfort in a place of caring. Monique was one of eleven children. Her father was a successful merchant, and her favorite memories are of the "Grande Maison," her parents' home. Monique's description of Haiti from those decades past is full of rich, vibrant colors. Not to be outdone by the natural beauty of the abundant tropical fruit and lush vegetation, Haitian women dressed in colorful clothes with every detail drawing attention to their own natural beauty. True beauty is also shown through a woman's hospitality and how she talks to others, Monique says. When asked if she reflects these characteristics she answers in her native French, "Oui!"

Monique's smile reflects the joy she feels from living each day surrounded by those she loves. Her happiest moments are when she is talking and laughing with her three children, who live nearby. They make this humble woman proud—humble enough to understand the importance of daily conversation with her Lord, but proud enough to boast of her children's achievements and successes.

What does Monique dream about? The same thing she prays for: to always stay with the Lord, to be with him and walk with him. The peace she finds from living that dream radiates from within. In any language, that translates to true beauty.

Free Spirit

ROSA DAVIS was expected to follow the traditional path of Guadalajara's women—marriage and motherhood. But she had other plans.

When she was ten years old Rosa moved, with her mother, from Mexico to Perris, California. When her mother married a United States citizen, Rosa knew they were there to stay, and she struggled with the shock. She had loved the city of Guadalajara, with many friends living within a stone's throw. It was hard for her to adjust to Perris, with the houses miles apart and with classmates who didn't speak her language. Rosa never felt at home in California, not even by the time she reached high school. "I hated my environment and did not feel balanced," Rosa says. "It is hard to feel pretty when you don't feel good inside."

Rosa graduated from high school at sixteen and married soon after. The relationship proved unhealthy and abusive, and eight years later, Rosa made the decision to leave her husband.

"It was hard because I cared for him, and I was afraid to be alone," she says. She had already developed a plan for independence, but it took eighteen months to put into practice. "I had put a little money aside and paid off all my debts, but I didn't make the final decision to leave until I talked to a counselor. She couldn't tell me what to do, but she did say, 'If it were me, I would not stay.' That validated my decision."

Rosa never went home from that counseling session. She left her job, too, and began working as an usher with the Cirque du Soleil. She has been traveling with the show ever since, finding her own transportation from town to town and living in whatever quarters she can find on a bus route to the circus tent. "I am beginning the Bohemian years," Rosa says. "When I am not at work, I write or play guitar. One day I will write a song."

Perhaps destiny had other plans for Rosa after all.

Voices / Voces

CANDY TORRES

I have two voices	Dos voces cantan en mi corazón
Stuck within my body	Bailando en mi alma
But	Érase una vez
For too many years	Una voz
One was silent	Que durmía
Awake!	¡Despérate!
Speak to me!	¡Háblame!
They don't always speak together	No muere en el silencio
One is the voice	Respire la vida de mi herencia
Of my mother	De mis padres, mis abuelos
Had she worked	Permítalos una vida nueva
On her poetry	En mi poesía
Her tongue sleeps	Prueba las palabras de la otra
In my heart	No más la voz sola
The other is mine	Hay dos lados de mi alma
The tongue of my life	Un secreto demasiado tiempo
No	Otra vez
Both are my life	Soy entera
My life needs both	Somos juntos
Together	Aun cuando
In harmony	Hablamos
And in opposite visions	En contra visiones
One was dominant	No más es una voz dominante
But now	Ahora
My voices, my tongues	Mis voces, mis lenguas
Two sides of my spirit	Dos lados de mi alma
Need to work	Necesitan trabajar
For the construction	Para construir
Reconstruction of	Reconstruir de
My dreams	Mis sueños
My life	Mi vida
Me	Mí

20

Skin Deep

MARY LAUFER

The authentic woman stands
in front of a mirror
and dwells on her imperfections:
She wishes her teeth were whiter,
her nose smaller, her breasts bigger,
her stomach flatter. If only the fat roll
at her waist would disappear.

She does two hundred crunches a day,
tries a low-carb diet, starves herself,
steps on the scale morning and night.
She buys underwire bras, bleaches her teeth,
still feels ugly, not good enough.
It costs a fortune to go under the knife:
nose job, liposuction, breast augmentation.
She will be beautiful, no matter the cost.

A month after surgery,
the superficial woman spends afternoons
in therapy staring into a mirror.
The fat roll at her waist has disappeared,
but so has she. Her humility is smaller,
her vanity bigger, her personality flatter.
If only she could remember how she felt
to be genuine, when she was more than
just something pretty to look at.

Animal Attraction

ROBIN LYON is living her childhood dream.

She has traded the glamorous life of a globehopping flight attendant for the daily routine of feeding and caring for more than eighty animals on the Lyon Ranch in California. Robin doesn't know exactly how many animals there are or how much the ranch spends on food and veterinarian bills. She never wants to turn an animal away for economic reasons; her daily decisions are driven by the question, "Am I making a difference?"

Robin bought twelve acres near her home in Napa, California, while working for Delta Airlines, determined to fulfill her dream, alone if she had to. Then, on a fateful flight, she fell in love with the pilot, Robert. That "city fellow" soon embraced Robin's dream. Today Robin, Robert, and their daughter, Lynette, spend their time nursing abandoned and neglected animals back to health. They also train animals for nursing home visits, and the most popular is a camel named Kazzy. Though Robin had to convince Robert that buying the 103-pound baby camel was a good idea, he now refers to Kazzy as *his* camel. Kazzy is even welcome in the lobby of the local bank, thanks to Robin's determination and intensive daily training.

Visiting the Lyon Ranch is like stepping into a fantasy world. Cats, even wild ones, live peacefully among birds of every color; dogs run among goats; donkeys frolic with camels. As Robin walks around the grounds, she has kind, soft words and gentle strokes for every animal, calling them all by name. The family does all the training, cleaning, and feeding, and conducts nursing home visits with little financial or in-kind help from others. Occasional offerings from churches and other groups, plus a small nonprofit discount on vet bills, helps them make ends meet.

"My dream was to make a better life for both the animals and the elderly," Robin says. "If I died tomorrow, I would feel like I am fulfilled. I wanted to make a difference, and I have."

Freedom

JOSÉE SIMBABAWE, a refugee from the war-torn country of Burundi, dreams of helping other refugees from the homeland she fled nine years ago.

Josée may never know the identity of everyone who worked to gain refugee status for her, but she owes them her freedom. She feels lucky to now live in Montreal, where she has been accepted and has many opportunities to better her own life and the lives of her family members back in Burundi.

She was not so lucky during the time she spent in Kenya, stranded between family and freedom. A Tutsi, Josée was arrested twice by opposition forces and once spent three days in a prison cell so crowded with other Tutsis that they had to take turns sitting in order to sleep. She refused to eat the filthy food that was provided, and drank little of the dirty water. "It was worse for the children," Josée says.

As she relates the horrors of war, passion darkens her black eyes, and an inner spark accentuates her physical beauty. Before the war, lush vegetation filled Burundi with beauty and friendly people filled it with laughter. Saddened by the way war has ravaged her country and its people, and thankful for her own improved situation, Josée now dreams of using her blessings to help those she left behind.

Despite vast changes in her homeland, Josée says the definition of a beautiful Burundi woman remains the same: tall, voluptuous and big-hipped. Josée admits she herself would not meet such expectations; perhaps that is why she has an unassuming style that exhibits simple elegance and ease.

Josée recognizes true beauty in people who accept others, without judgment. "We do not know anything about the big picture," she says. "We do not know anything about what is going on in their lives." Her knowledge of the ways of the world, ways of life, and ways of people creates an inner beauty in her that would find a home in any culture.

Victor

LESLEY PARROTT suffered a loss no mother should have to endure.

In 1986 she had it all—a rewarding advertising career in Toronto, a country farm, a city house, and a peaceful life with her husband, son, and daughter. Then one day, her eleven-year-old daughter, Allison, failed to come home from a track team photo shoot. Two days later the girl's body was found. It took ten years and twenty-two detectives to find the murderer. A match of DNA taken from semen samples at the scene proved his guilt.

"It was a loss of innocence," Lesley says. "I can never have that moment of absolute peace and serenity, because if I do, it gets snatched away."

For a long time Lesley had no will to live. For many years she would get angry at any signs of beauty and wonder how flowers had the nerve to bloom every spring. But Lesley never focused on the murderer. She always understood that he was a very sick man. "It has been important for me from the very beginning not to be caught up with revenge. I represent Allison to the world with love and vitality," Lesley says.

Ironically, Lesley played an instrumental role, the year after Allison's murder, in opposing a bill to reinstate capital punishment in Canada. "I had always been very anti-capital punishment and I became even more so. It is just the wrong thing to do."

Born a "Daughter of the Manse" in Scotland, Lesley learned organizational and counseling skills from her preacher father. She left high school at fifteen due to a learning disability and took a secretarial job in Toronto, where she met the man to whom she has been married for twenty-eight years. By the age of nineteen, she was producing commercials. Today, she still works in advertising, but also counsels others through Bereaved Families of Ontario (which she directs) and Stay Alert, Stay Safe (which she founded with other advertising executives). Helping others work through grief gives her life meaning.

"In order to survive a tragedy of this magnitude, that completely shakes your belief in the goodness of life, you have to be yourself," Lesley says. "I don't consider myself a victim. I am a victor."

Enlightenment

TOMIKO LALONDE knows what it is like to come up from the depths of darkness—despair so deep that she once contemplated suicide.

She was a young mother struggling to raise two daughters. Her desire to be a good parent conflicted with her own childhood memories of the harsh words, strict discipline, and abuse she had suffered at the hands of her father. Her parents, who had emigrated from Japan, had moved the family to Alberta, Canada, after World War II to escape persecution.

tomiko's parents were farm workers. The children of other local families spent their days in school, but during harvest time tomiko's father demanded that his children help him in the fields. Tears fill tomiko's eyes as she describes twelve-hour days cutting and stacking large bunches of sugar beets. She was six years old, a small child.

Her tearful eyes turn dark and defiant as she remembers the time she dared to talk back to her father, whom she describes as "a genius gone mad." She then went to her room and waited, expecting him to come and kill her—such was her fear of the one who should have been providing security and comfort.

Years later, tomiko did not carry through on her thoughts of suicide because she could bear neither to leave her children without a mother nor to take them with her. Her only option was to begin the long climb out of darkness by resolving the inner turmoil only she was aware of. She embarked on a journey of healing, and along the way she discovered her true spiritual, emotional, and intellectual strength. Today, tomiko shares her wisdom with many young people who e-mail her daily. Many of those she advises come to stay at her pristine home while on their own personal journeys.

tomiko rejects such conventional traditions as observing birthdays, capitalizing her first name, or marrying her boyfriend, who is twenty years her junior. She values truth above all else and celebrates each day with an attitude of thanks.

"I'm the ugly duckling," tomiko says. "I found my inner beauty and became a swan. I'm the luckiest girl on the planet."

Nature's Child

JOAN COBB-BEAUMONT exudes natural beauty: What you see is what you get.

She admits her choice to forego makeup often makes her feel like an outsider, but she resists the temptation to conform to others' ideas of beauty. She lives life at "face value," dismissing unrealistic expectations and wasteful jealousy and instead choosing to be true to the person she is. Spending time with Joan brings thoughts of the "Peace, Love and Rock and Roll" mood of the 1960s. She is a bit young to have lived that decade except as a small child, but her life mirrors the ideals of that age, including the belief that we are all beautiful on the inside.

Joan is passionate about art, music, and nature. She puts her college degree to work in a stained glass studio, and satisfies her desire to perform by playing the flute at charitable events and by singing in church and at weddings. Nestled among the thriving plants that fill her home are leaves, feathers, and rocks she has collected since childhood.

Joan took off to see the world when she finished school, traveling with only a tent to separate her from the natural world she loved. Her journey brought her to Calgary in 1981. She planned to stay just a short while, but that changed when she met her future husband. Today, they have created a loving home for their daughter and son. Their lives are simple and free from the demands of a materialistic world. Family conversations are filled with laughter as they share memories of camping and traveling together. Each member is encouraged to pursue his or her dream, whether it is pottery, art, painting, writing, or exploring the world.

Joan dreams of living in a simple cabin in the wild without electricity, spending all her spare time on artistic pursuits. That dream is on hold until her children set off on their own, hopefully filled with the knowledge that they each have something special to share with the world. "I am happy to be patient and live for the now," Joan says, adding there is a time for everything. "We all have things that makes us beautiful. Our purpose is to share our gifts."

Success

ISABELLA FU believes her childhood struggles have made her stronger.

"People who have struggled at a young age are fortunate because they know they have conquered it," Isabella says. "It teaches you to have an independent spirit."

Growing up Asian in the southwestern United States was difficult for Isabella and a painful physical ailment compounded her life. Her father died when she was seven; afterward, the family moved from state to state as her engineer mother worked to raise three small children. Isabella's parents, born in China, had always discouraged their children from speaking Chinese. Yet despite speaking perfect English, Isabella was very conscious of being different and had few friends in school. But she excelled academically despite the social challenges. A physics degree from Radcliffe, a law degree from Columbia, and a successful job at Intel helped Isabella land her current job at Microsoft. She took a cut in pay to make the career move so she could return to her love of practicing law.

"I don't really care about what my title is," Isabella says. "A lot of people don't ever figure out what is important to them. To go through life with a lack of joy, that is sad."

Isabella has plenty to feel joyful about. After a challenging day at work she enjoys spending evenings in her waterfront condominium, looking through the floor-to-ceiling windows at Seattle's skyline. Her home is filled with works of local artists and with photographs she has taken during travels around the world.

Isabella devotes her free time to her "little sister" in the Big Brothers/Big Sisters program and to hiking, biking, and swimming. The same physical ailment she suffered as a youth has recently forced her to quit jogging, and the situation may get worse as she grows older, but she refuses to become a victim. Instead, Isabella focuses on the things that are important to her—a rewarding job, giving to the community, and a comfortable home. Isabella also says she prefers to date younger men because they accept her success more easily than do men her own age.

"They can let their egos out of it," Isabella says, adding that dating is not her top priority. "At the end of the day, it hasn't been that important to get married or have kids, but it is something that is missing from my life."

Advocacy

KARIN MENG believes in using her talents and abilities to help others.

Her latest cause is educating people about the challenges faced by the visually impaired. Karen, an ophthalmologist, recently produced a public service announcement with one of her patients. The announcement is now airing on television stations in the California Bay Area, reminding sighted persons and drivers to be considerate of all types of vision difficulties. "That is my new juice," Karin says. "I am a low-vision advocate."

Karin is energetic, positive and enjoys laughter—all traits that have served her well during tough times. A few years ago, her ex-husband was diagnosed with lung cancer. Karin realized the importance of surrounding him with peace, harmony, and family, so she devoted eighteen months to caring for him during his last days. She began to study spirituality as related to death and dying. Her relationship with her son, who was thirteen when his father died, deepened. But her act of boundless love had been for her ex-husband as well as for her son. "I decided we were all going to get along," Karin says. "I made sure there was peace. I feel good about it every day."

Karin admits that when she was young, she didn't feel she fit in. Her intelligence, frizzy hair, "goofy" sense of humor, bad complexion, and glasses all added up to, in Karin's words, a "memorizing egg-headed girl." Her family used to call her "dicke," or "fatty" in her native language of German, but Karin soon discovered that exercise, yoga, and healthy eating helped her inner beauty shine. She now knows that discovering who you are is much more beautiful than trying to be like others. "I used to blame Cher for my unhappiness," says Karin, who now has a new take on beauty. "Everyone's differences are what are beautiful. You can tell a beautiful woman by her eyes. It would be great if we all looked the way we truly are."

Karin embodies that ideal. She is a beautiful and caring advocate at peace with her place in the world.

She May Be Found

NANCY GUSTAFSON

She may be found
    on hands and knees in a flower bed,
    trowel in hand, hair stuck to sweat
    on her brow, face smudged with dirt;
And next year
    green stems will break through soil
    to reach for the sky, buds will swell
    and unfurl their faces to the sun.

She may be found
    in a rocking chair, baby cradled
    in her arms, tiny head on her breast,
    with spit-up on her shirt;
And years from now
    children will break through adolescence,
    reach their arms to embrace a needy world
    and turn their faces heavenward.

She may be found
    at the kitchen sink washing dishes,
    caring for a sick loved-one, steadfastly
    standing by family through life's trials;
And years from now
    in God's own time, her family
    will reach toward her with grateful arms
    and smile into her remarkable face.

The House Dress

SUE MAYFIELD-GEIGER

My first view of her every morning was the calves of her legs –
solid and tanned –
as she stood at the kitchen sink with her hands
and arms buried in the pink Vel dishwater.
The hem of her housedress swayed below her knees.
Tiny floral designs lived on the pale blue one;
stripes of gray lived on the other.

I knew both garments by heart.
Cotton, worn and faded,
a Sears tag dangling backside,
sleeveless, two skirt pockets,
one slightly torn.
Sturdy upper arms, brown like her calves,
bounced in unison.
"It's cause I'm big-boned," she'd laugh.

Big-boned hands baked pineapple pies, waxed
wooden floors, and embraced rich, clay gumbo,
planting a backyard garden of pansies, snapdragons,
rose bushes, honeysuckle, cockscomb, sweet peas,
morning glories, petunias and ferns.
I learned all their names as she identified
each one at feeding time.
Red bricks kept them in perfect alignment.

Two frayed housedresses bear a lifetime
of suds and dirt while delicate flowers within
the confines of symmetric borders flourished.
And one big-boned woman
Passed secrets on to her daughter.

Independence

EDNA SHINN was thirteen when the Great Depression hit in 1929. She subsequently quit school to work at Eiband's Department Store, on Postoffice Street in Galveston, Texas.

Six years later President Roosevelt's initiatives doubled her salary to twelve dollars per week and allowed her to take one day a week off. "I've been a Democrat ever since," Edna says.

In 1938, Edna married Clarence Shinn. She says the toughest times were when they were newlyweds and Clarence was making thirteen dollars per week, less than twice the cost of rent. There wasn't much take-home pay left after transportation costs and taxes. Somehow they managed, despite complications during the birth of their son less than a year after they were married. They couldn't afford hospitalization, so a relative cared for Edna and her son. He developed whooping cough and the young family's struggles worsened. When a baby girl arrived a few years later, the family was living in a tiny apartment and sharing a bathroom with six other families. It was 1949 before they could buy a house of their own.

After 61 years of marriage, Clarence died of Alzheimer's disease complications, and Edna suddenly found herself alone. She chose to remain in the family house, and says she gets angry when someone tries to convince her to spend a night away from her home. "I am happy being independent," she says. That doesn't mean she stays at home. Edna, who has never had a driver's license, is grateful to friends who bring her to the grocery store and to church every week. Her favorite memories include the long trips she and Clarence used to take, especially the Hawaiian vacation for their fiftieth wedding anniversary.

On the wall above her bed is a tapestry of an angel. It reminds her of the angel that appeared to her a few weeks after her husband died. Although her startled reaction scared the vision away, she believes it was a sign that her husband was watching over her. That memory gives her peace, and when Edna smiles, an indomitable spirit of independence and faith radiates from within.

Communicator

NELLIE CHAPPELL-WHITE knows how to communicate in any situation.

She was raised in a Texas military town with a generous mix of cultures. Even so, Nellie says there was a "Barbie doll" ideal. Her strict father did not allow her to date in high school, so she wrote a long note to tell Tyrone, the class clown and star athlete, that she admired him. Her friends thought she was crazy, but her method of communication worked. Nellie and Tyrone are still together, working side by side to create a good home and family life for their daughter, Taryn. "When you have confidence enough in yourself to tell the truth no matter what, and not back down, you have inner beauty," Nellie says. "Beauty in general is very oversold."

Nellie's confidence has served her well. She recently created a radio talk show, "Focus on Personal Growth," that airs bi-weekly on Houston Pacifica radio, 90.1 FM. She has no trouble finding guests to talk about positive things they are involved in locally. "There is so much to people," Nellie says. "When you sit down and talk to them, they are so interesting."

Nellie has always been shocked and surprised when confronted with prejudice, no matter where it comes from. She is bothered by preconceived notions and people who refuse to accept others on an individual basis. "I feel passionate about people accepting each other," Nellie says. "I try to meet a lot of people. It is nice to hear their stories and learn from them."

Her talk show encourages listeners to achieve their best by making positive changes in their lives. She also provides a forum for guests to present useful and insightful information on how to achieve goals. "Living an average life is easy; take chances and see what really drives you," Nellie says.

The tagline for her show sums up her own journey: "Aim beyond your reach."

Artistic Vision

KETRA OBERLANDER has, ironically, chosen painting to express her frustration at living in a visual world that is increasingly closed to her.

Ketra was born with cone dystrophy, a genetic condition that affects her day vision and her ability to see color and fine detail. For years, she gave little thought to the possibility that her vision would deteriorate to the point of blindness, but as her cone dystrophy has progressed, it has become very difficult for her to see much of anything. "It is very frustrating," Ketra says. "We live in a sight-oriented society."

After finding success as a writer and a popular sex humorist, she moved from Kansas City to San Francisco in 1996 because San Francisco was one of the top five publishing markets—and because it had a good public transportation system. Ketra recently made her decision to stop writing and turn to painting. "Language was failing me," she says. "It was no longer a good medium to express my deep personal frustration. I feel like I've said everything I have wanted to say." Now, she uses a "visual fill-in-the-blank" approach as she paints, working at a close distance and guessing at the colors she chooses. Ketra is passionate about the message her paintings convey. "It is my goal, through my work, to reflect the art of possibility," Ketra says. "It may not be huge or monumental, but it absolutely changes the world. If I can do this with diminishing sight, you, too, can express whatever you are going through, which is most temporary."

Ketra enjoys gourmet cooking, she says because she enjoys gourmet eating. What may be a pleasant hobby for some presents an added challenge for Ketra. She has to constantly travel back and forth from her kitchen to her living room to read the recipes, because she can only see the text when it is projected onto a magnified television screen. Her condition also complicates other tasks many of us take for granted. She must make advance arrangements for "spontaneous" trips into town, and go equipped with a telescope, magnifier, special sunglasses, and a white-tipped cane. "I don't expect to be treated gingerly, but I do expect the help I need," Ketra says. "It's an adjustment, but it is not extraordinary."

Ketra's positive attitude has turned her visual challenge into an artistic vision that many can enjoy. Her paintings can be seen at www.droolingcat.com.

Healer

El March, born Fatemeh El Tayebotahcr, fled Iran for Canada in 1979, when the Shah was overthrown.

As a child, El was fascinated with needles, amazed that medicine could be delivered to the body in that manner. Her dolls soon were full of holes from her "practice" sessions. She had completed twenty-four years' worth of schooling by the time she was eighteen, and had received a Ph.D. in orthomolecular medicine (an alternative approach to curing diseases, by working on the molecular level). Soon after she graduated, her mother was diagnosed with cancer and given just a few months to live. El put her on a treatment program that began with a change of attitude and diet. Twenty-six years later, her mother is still alive—and married to a man twenty-five years younger.

When El was a young girl, her two sisters and a brother were tragically killed in an accident. Her only surviving sibling, an older brother, became a Supreme Court Justice under the Shah's rule. He fled to Germany after the coup and, like El, chose not to return to Iran. "When I left, I thought I would never go back," El says. She settled in Toronto and began a counseling service that focused on the physical aspects of orthomolecular medicine. Today, she has developed fifty health products, which she sells through her company, Elaliance, Incorporated. She has also written two books, *Miracles in Now* and *It's All Up to You.* "I am most proud of helping people," El says. "I am blessed with that."

When she was thirteen, her mother told her she had to pick something to believe in. Her family was Muslim and she had read the Koran dozens of times, but she began to study the world's other religions. Eventually, when her mother asked her what religion she had decided to believe in, El answered, "My own," an answer that was true to her individuality and her name. "El" is a Turkish nickname meaning "helping hands"; she changed her last name to "March" because to her that month stands for beginnings—the month she celebrates her birthday and the month she moved to Canada.

"Wherever I am, that is my home," El says.

Hope

ELIZABETH TREVIÑO has never given up hope—not even when she was a ninety-pound prostitute eating from garbage cans, not even after she broke both legs jumping out of a third-story window to escape a would-be rapist.

That hope is what helped her overcome her addiction to crack cocaine.

Today, Elizabeth is a straight-A student at Alvin Community College in Texas, working to become a Licensed Chemical Dependency Counselor. She and her husband, Marvin, face daily struggles to make ends meet. But Elizabeth stays at the top of her class while taking up to twenty-three credit hours per semester and holding down a full-time, non-paying internship with the Council On Substance Abuse in Angleton, Texas. "I'm not asking anyone for anything," Elizabeth says. "I am strong, independent, and not fearful, because what doesn't kill me will make me stronger."

Her upbeat attitude, in the face of monumental financial and legal struggles, shows in her smile and her words. Elizabeth is very thankful for her children, Marvin, and her health. She believes she is in complete remission from her addiction, and says it is a miracle she came through the other side a whole and complete person. "Life is wonderful, regardless of the struggles," Elizabeth says. "I love to live and I like being me." Her children are the driving force behind her desire to work hard; she wants to provide a better life for them. They feed the flame of her passion to stay clean and to help others do the same by spreading the message of hope.

Some say there are three ends to drug addiction: jail; institutionalization; or death. For Elizabeth, hope has led to a fourth, better end: working toward her dream of living happily with her family and adding financial health to her list of blessings. The hope she embodies has given her the strength to improve her life through education and determination, making her a courageous and truly beautiful woman.

"I am proud of the person I have become," Elizabeth says. "I can do anything I want. I am empowered, and I think that is a beautiful thing."

Square Peg

never thought she was gay; she just thought she didn't fit in.

After college she had married a man she loved. When they began to have sexual problems, therapy revealed repressed memories of childhood sexual abuse by her father and began to illuminate her own sexual orientation. While looking at a book describing sexual fantasies, Hellen suddenly realized only one had any effect on her—the one showing two women together. She knew she had found the missing link to love in her life. Her husband had been very supportive, but their marriage could not survive that hurdle.

Today, Hellen has made a new life for herself and fits right in as co-president of the Board of Directors of the Lesbian Gay Bi-Sexual Transgender Community Center in Seattle. She now has a strong sense of belonging, but admits she likes to stand out, even in her current role. "I like reclaiming the drag queen and campiness in women," she says, describing the evening gowns she wore at a recent fundraiser for the center. "I like to be a bit outrageous for such events, even to the point of taking on a different persona."

Hellen is dedicated to whatever cause she takes on, whether overseeing the board activity for the community center or working as an occupational therapist for special education children. She has made a decision to always give her all. "I am proud to know what it means to give one hundred percent," Hellen says, adding that she is finally seeing the fruits of her efforts. "I am becoming the type of board president that all organizations like mine need."

Hellen is spiritual, passionate, and pensive. Her mom taught her and her twin sister the skills of Transcendental Meditation when they were young. Hellen enjoys riding her 1999 Triumph Legend motorcycle and going downhill skiing. She strives to be like the people she admires, living out loud, doing versus not doing, and saying versus not saying. She now speaks openly about the abuse she and her sister suffered at the hands of their father, who died fifteen years ago. "If it is aired out, there is less of a dynamic of secrecy to help the perpetrator," Hellen says. "The shame should not reside with the victim."

Whether speaking openly about abuse or speaking out for the LGBT Community Center, Hellen has found a niche that fits her perfectly.

Training Day

Lisa E. Beatman

It was my birthday – nine! years! old! I'd blown out all the candles with the help of my ratfink brothers, and made a wish. The floor was all jumbled with paper and pigtails of ribbon. I'd unwrapped all the presents but one. Auntie Francy said leave that till last. There was Malibu Barbie and Betsy Wetsy, since I still didn't know where I was heading, and Barbie had such cool clothes but Betsy Wetsy had a tummy and flat feet and her I could relate to. There was Twister and Chutes and Ladders, 'cos I still wasn't sure which way I was going and I loved belly flopping head first down the slide at school, but Ann who babysat us played Twister with her boyfriend when we were supposed to be in bed, and I wanted a boyfriend someday just like him. There was a bottle of bubble bath and a bottle of toilet water since I still didn't know where I was heading and I still adored squeaky toys in the bath, but Mommy smelled so pretty on Saturday nights and I wanted to grow up to smell just like her.

There was layer cake and ice cream, vanilla and marble swirl, and finally Auntie Francy said ok now, you can open my gift. I tried to take the tape off without tearing the shiny paper. I'd ripped open all the others, but Auntie Mimi said save the paper. I still didn't know where I was going and maybe you needed extra paper when you got there. The box was flat and inside there were layers of white tissue paper and inside the tissue paper was a strip of white ruffles. I held it up and it was this wide and had straps this narrow and Auntie Mimi said why it's a training bra and Uncle Arthur said what's she training for and Mommy just smiled. Auntie Francy said go try it on so I went in the coat closet and pulled my tee shirt over my head and pulled the white lace down around my chest. It had a hook and eyelet in the back, and in front, no cups at all. I liked how the satin felt, cool and slidey, but wasn't at all sure about the elastic. It was a new experience.

I opened the closet door out into the hot spotlight of grown-up expectations. The applause was intoxicating. Tiny rows of ruffles made my chest stick out a bit, or was it pride, or imagination, or the giddy rush of standing on the edge of something really huge? I hugged my slippery chest and pranced around the center ring. It's a size 22, I got it a little big — she'll grow into it, Auntie Francy said. Grow into what, I said and spun around, a silly bean? I spun and spun, till the giggles wove themselves into a tall green lattice I climbed up till I was dizzy and collapsed on the specked shag rug. My face was wet, and I couldn't catch my breath. Daddy said ok Miss Ballerina it's off with you to the Featherbed Ball.

Well, turns out I never did grow into it, really, the cups, the elastic, the white satin promise. I'm still in training, I guess, and mom's still smiling, from somewhere.

Mom, too, was flat as a pancake, and nursed all four of us thank you ma'am. Everything I have works, and nothing sags. Auntie Francy had a mastectomy last year, and now sports a prostheses she calls Vera. It flops on the bed when I help her off with it, and I flop beside it, talking of things Aunties and nieces talk about; chemotherapy, my partner or lack thereof, and the formative role in a girl's life played by foundation garments, the fragile silk, the tough elastic, the intricate lace.

Mental Health

SARAH BYAM lives on a promise that she will call for help if she ever has thoughts of suicide again.

In the past, friends often remained on the phone with her until she calmed down. She describes how her husband David has had to gently pull her by the wrists from under a piece of furniture and "into the light." She credits her current state of mental health to David and to a doctor who helped her break the downward-spiraling cycle of depression. Sarah is now committed to lifelong treatment for a chemical imbalance that causes depression and mood swings.

She likens her childhood environment to a concentration camp ruled by her authoritarian stepmother who believed Sarah was an evil child whose ego was destroying the marriage. "To learn that was not true was the biggest challenge I had to overcome," Sarah says. "My only sin was that I wanted to live." Sarah was beaten when her household chores did not pass inspection. She was forbidden to sing, listen to the radio, watch television, read, or own anything. Even her food and water were rationed. It took Sarah a long time to forgive her Native American mother for not coming to take her away. "I never asked to get out, but I did ask for strength and sometimes I asked for relief," Sarah says. "My experiences have made me strong; they have given me a great capacity for compassion and love for my fellow man."

At the age of fifteen, Sarah was placed in a foster home where she had a room of her own, clothes, and food, all luxuries to her. That was the first step of a long and continuing journey toward mental stability. She still takes eight medications daily to treat manic-depression, post-traumatic stress, anxiety, and obsessive-compulsive and sleep disorders, but she chooses to focus on the positive aspects of her life. And she has learned to share strength with others. Her monthly column on www.tuppenceworth.ie has thousands of readers. Her graphic novel about a girl superhero, *Billi 99,* is in its second printing and has been translated into four languages. She and David are now writing a book together. Sarah finally has the love, stability, and security she was denied in childhood.

"You don't get love by grabbing for it, you get love by giving love," Sarah says. "I have another forty or fifty years left to do whatever I want. I am at peace."

Earth Mother

HUGUETTE VERVROEGEN is a nurturer in every sense of the word.

As a neonatal nurse at Montreal Jewish Hospital, she cares for the frailest and tiniest babies, the ones struggling just to take a breath. She talks softly to them as she gently cradles them in one hand, often with worried parents looking on. At home on her farm, she cares for animals and tends to various vegetable crops that are sold locally. Huguette loves to sit on her porch, looking out over the fields of freshly harvested hay as the sun goes down. Horses dot the pasture, geese honk near a pond, and kittens mew from the greenhouse nearby. Huguette's deeply caring attitude for all things living is obvious whether she is tending crops, feeding animals, or working in the neonatal unit.

Huguette sees beyond physical beauty, recognizing value in people on a level that goes much deeper than the visible. "Thank God it is like that, because otherwise, everyone would go for the same man or woman," Huguette says, adding that her boyfriend of many years is the best man in the world. "I see beauty in people that eyes cannot see."

Passion and joy radiating from within define Huguette's own beauty, but to her a beautiful woman is one who "speaks her soul," who has learned to trust her truest self through struggle. Huguette admits she would like to be more childlike, living in the present moment without a thought of past or future. One day she hopes to overcome her fear of flying and travel to other nations to help vaccinate children. For now, her family, including a daughter and a grandson, depends on her.

"I am a fighter for others and against injustice," Huguette says. "We don't do enough. Our lives are so empty. Children die because there is no food, or they die from disease, and what we do? Nothing! This is killing me."

Bravery

Denyse Deschênes has worn dentures since she was sixteen years old.

Her mother had Denyse's teeth pulled because it cost less than having them filled or straightened. Denyse recently underwent painful oral surgery to have new teeth implanted; a bone graft (from her own hip) was also necessary, because part of her upper gum had been damaged by wearing dentures for more than forty years, and had to be replaced.

"I wanted to get rid of that foreign object in my mouth," Denyse said. "I could not taste or feel the texture of food because the dentures covered my palate. I can taste food now."

Denyse gets tears in her eyes when she talks about her mom, now deceased. She says she loved her mother very much, but didn't like her. Physical scars remain from the abuse Denyse suffered at the hands of her mother. Ironically, her younger brother was spared such abuse. At the age of eighteen, she married—into another abusive relationship—to get away from her home in Labrador City, Newfoundland. Two sons and eleven years later, she decided she had to leave, but it wasn't any easier than the first time she fled home. "As I drove away, I watched the black spruce trees disappear in the rearview mirror," Denyse says. "I looked ahead to the maple trees coming at me, and I thought, 'I'm free!'"

That freedom came with a price. Denyse faced the toughest time of her life as she struggled to raise her sons on her own. She believes a guardian angel was watching out for her and helped lead her to better times: "I'm a firm believer that there is somebody up there looking after me, and that there is a reason for everything I go through."

Today, her life is filled with happiness and love. Denyse and her partner, Bob, recently remodeled the home they have shared for more than twenty years, to accommodate his mother, who has Alzheimer's disease. Helping to care for Bob's mother has taught Denyse a lot about herself, as her patience and compassion is tested on a daily basis. "I still don't feel as if I have found my inner beauty," Denyse says. "But I have strength and if I put my mind to anything, it gets done."

Imperfection

LISA MCCLEOD can laugh at herself for her imperfections.

When she speaks to women on her philosophy of life, described in her book, *Forget Perfect,* Lisa wears a "Queen of Perfect" crown and white gloves to put priorities in the proper perspective.

There was a time when Lisa fell into the perfection trap like so many women do. For years, she spent valuable time on trivial things, rather than the things which really matter—creating happy memories in the family and developing true friendships. Lisa was jerked away from the elusive lure of perfection at her mother's funeral, when she realized the woman being eulogized as a community activist did not have one true friend present. Lisa says her mom avoided getting too close to people, settling for numerous working relationships through the organizations and activities that demanded her time. That funeral provided a life-defining moment for Lisa when she realized there is more to life than just "doing."

"'Forget perfect' doesn't mean lowering your standards; it means raising them for what really matters," Lisa later wrote in her book. "Perfect doesn't last, friends do."

Today, she asks her seminar participants what they want their lives to be like. Then, she asks them how they want to feel. Lisa says there is inevitably a gap between the two, and the first step toward closing it is realizing what you have. "People are desperately craving outer perfection because they are blind to inner perfection," Lisa says, admitting that same drive kept her from recognizing her own beauty while growing up. Now, when she looks at old photos, she realizes she was beautiful. "I have never felt beautiful. I think that is a shame."

Lisa says everybody has a drive to improve, but it makes her feel sad and annoyed when she sees women wasting time trying to be people they are not. Lisa admits she has been guilty of the same habit in the past.

"A beautiful woman is someone who glows from inside and is comfortable with how she looks, imperfections and all—a woman who has sparkles in her eyes," Lisa says. "On a good day, I am that woman."

Overlooked Beauty

Yaffa Tsadyk has always been beautiful, but she didn't think so for a long time.

When she was a child in Russia, a photographer came to her school, which was celebrating the opening of a new building. Yaffa was selected from her class to be photographed, but when the big day came, another girl's photo appeared in the place of hers. Yaffa painfully assumed it was because she was not pretty enough. Years later, her father told her that he believed the real reason she was denied her moment of glory was that Yaffa was a Hebrew name. Even he, who had been used to "the system," was shocked at such anti-Semitism.

Yaffa and her husband came to the United States eighteen years ago from what is now Uzbekistan, seeking job opportunities. He had been a pharmacist and she a teacher, but she never pursued teaching in the United States because of the language barrier, though she had hoped to open a day care center. Instead, she began working at the Dyanna beauty salon in New York City. Soon a customer, Cheryl, began encouraging Yaffa to learn English and bringing note cards with new words every week. Yaffa fondly remembers Cheryl's acceptance and encouragement: "It was beautiful." Before Cheryl came along to help, Yaffa was often at a loss for words: "I tried to pretend that I understood."

Yaffa now has a new dream: to travel throughout the world with her husband when he retires. Until then, she will continue to do the things she loves, spending time with her family and working at the salon. She is proud of her two sons, who both hold MBAs; of her three grandsons; and of her work.

"My grandsons are my passion, but I can't imagine sitting at home just watching TV or taking care of them," Yaffa says. "I like to meet people. I like to make people happy and help them look good."

Meditation

GABRIELE HILBERG has embarked on a journey of self-discovery very few of us would be willing to undertake.

It began in 1986, when she closed her office for forty days and went to Maui, Hawaii, to meditate. During that time, she lived on water and minerals and broke all communication ties – no television, radio, telephone or computer. She denied herself even the simple pleasures of reading and writing, except for thirty minutes of dictation each night which she saved for her secretary to transcribe upon her return. Her days consisted of "sitting on a patch of ground" and just listening. On the thirty-fourth day, she took off her watch. By the thirty-sixth day, she was about to give up: "I thought, 'This is the strangest vacation I have ever been on and I haven't had any fun yet.'" But in the next moment, she had a revelation, "a deep spiritual recognition that everything is related to a larger order." Today, her spiritual awareness shapes her counseling more than her educational background does.

Gabriele grew up in Düsseldorf, Germany. Undiagnosed learning disabilities made school a challenge, but she worked hard to become a teacher like her older sister. Today she has three master's degrees and a Ph.D. "I grew up with very little identity," Gabriele says. "As a kid, I wasn't anything special."

Her classmates, who often turned to her for advice, may have disagreed. When she was fifteen, she began to schedule counseling sessions during recess. Unknown to her teachers, she arranged late night discussion groups during overnight field trips. It was only after several college professors requested appointments with her that she realized her gift for counseling.

Gabriele spent twenty-eight years on her education and has taught in sixteen different countries. She facilitates "Think Lab," a local weekly discussion group. During a recent meeting, Gabriele skillfully facilitated a heady discussion of how many people have been conditioned to believe the external world is more real than the internal world, and may consciously create their own realities based on what is most self-serving.

Revelations from sitting on that patch of ground in Hawaii, meditation, and honoring the intuitive mind have made Gabriele the beautiful woman she is.

Identity

CAROLINA LOREN finally knows who she is.

Growing up, she frequently had strong, unidentified feelings involving two names she heard often, Ivy and Raymond. Comments from her aunt about how different Carolina was from her siblings added to the confusion. "I hated me," Carolina says. "I hated being black. I would stay in white circles and even now, I have very few friends who are black."

When she was eighteen she hitchhiked to Toronto and rented a room in a boarding house for twenty dollars a week. She got a job as a nurse's aide and began a life of self-education. But even after her children were born, a sense of identity continued to elude her. Her stepfather suggested she write down everything she was good at and, after looking at her list, advised her to become a literary agent. She began meeting with agents in New York City to learn everything she could about the business, and noticed a trend toward self-publishing. Authors were soon approaching her, asking for help publishing their own books with the "big house" look. So she started The Natural Wellness Group, a company that provides printing, marketing, publishing, and promotional services.

After her mother died four years ago, Carolina found an entry for Ivy and Raymond in her mother's address book. Carolina wrote to them in England, hoping to find out why hearing those two names had always meant so much. Within days, she received a reply from Raymond, who said he was so happy to have found his "Little Carolina." She learned that her mother had conceived her out of wedlock in Jamaica and, facing ostracism by a strict culture, had given the infant to this white English couple. Carolina was returned to her mother at the age of four, shortly before her family moved to London, Ontario.

A photograph on her mantel shows baby Carolina in the arms of Ivy and Raymond. They sent it to her after they learned where she was. It represents a past she has no memory of, but she knows what the future holds.

"My journey is just beginning. Everything I have done in my life up to now has led to this," Carolina says. "My passion is health and wellness. My mission right now is to spend the next ten years of my life making a difference."

Black Women, Tired

ROLANDA PYLE

Black Women, Tired
Black Women, Tired
Years of Tiredness
      Fighting, pushing, hoping
Tired!

Slavery, freedom, wifehood, motherhood
Tired!

Losing our identities and our children,
Tired!

Possessing years of tired!
  Our grandmothers' tired,
    Our ancestors' tired,
      Sojourner Truth's tired,
        Rosa Parks' tired,
          Winnie Mandela's tired!
All rolled up into one Tired!

Working in the fields,
Cleaning their houses,
Caring for their children,
Cooking their meals,

Rearing our children,
Supporting our men,
Holding together our families,
Helping our people,
Tired!

Can't you see it in our faces?
Don't you hear it in our voices?
We can feel it in our shoulders,
Tired! Tired! Tired!

But we rise up
We stand tall
We march on
We work on
We carry on!

We overcome our tired!
We don't let tired keep us down!
We can't let tired keep us down!

Can't you see it in our dancing?
Don't you hear it in our singing?
We can feel it in our living!
Victory! Victory! Victory!

We replace our Tired with Victory!
Years of Victory!
  Our grandmothers' victory
    Our ancestors' victory,
      Harriet Tubman's victory,
        Marva Collins' victory
          Maya Angelou's victory!
All rolled up into one . . . Victory!

Black Women, Victorious!
Black Women, Victorious!
Years of Victory
      Fighting, pushing, hoping
Victory!

Pretty

MARION DEUTSCHE COHEN

The first time I looked in the mirror
I mean specifically looked
at me, not the mirror
I mean the first time I looked in the mirror and asked,
    not "Do I exist?"
but "Am I pretty?"

I didn't particularly CARE whether or not I was pretty.
It was just that I'd seen movies where it had been
    asked of various girls, "Is she pretty?"
So I'd decided to ask, "Am I pretty?"
I thought pretty meant blonde hair (YELLOW hair)
thick curvy lips
long eyelashes
and eyebrows as opposed to eyebrow-segments.
I thought pretty meant a certain age range
late teens, early 20s
not eleven.

So I answered, "No,
I'm not pretty."
What I meant was, I'm not fancy.
And I knew I wasn't ugly, knew I wasn't gross.
And again, I didn't MIND not being pretty.
It was a matter-of-fact question, with a matter-of-fact
    answer.
"Am I pretty?" like "What time is it?"
It was a test question, a math problem.
Any answer was acceptable.

But I do remember that mirror.
The brown hair, brown eyes
all that brown and flesh, not much color.
And those square-upon-square inches of flat
    unillustrated skin.
Also, I didn't turn my head
so I didn't know I had high cheekbones and an
    aquiline nose.
"What a boring face," I thought, "what a wasteland."

But I didn't care.
It didn't matter.
I just went around for awhile, knowing I wasn't
    pretty.
Or: I went around not-knowing I was pretty.
Or: I went around knowing what I looked like, but
    nothing about it.
I just went around for awhile.
I just went around.

Intentional Life

GAIL EVANS went to work as a freelancer for a new television station in 1980, not knowing it was the beginning of a long and rewarding career.

"Nobody had any idea how big CNN would become," Gail says. "Life will lead you where you need to be, if you show up."

She had started an international consulting and public relations company, Global Research Services, after the birth of her third child. The freelance work she did for CNN soon led to a full-time job offer; eventually, she became an executive vice president to whom all talk shows reported. Her department was responsible for scheduling 25,000 interviews per year. Despite her stressful job, she was always able to turn her mind off when she needed a break, though she preferred to take one or two days off at a time instead of long vacations. At the age of fifty, she bought an Arabian horse to resume a riding hobby she had enjoyed as a child. Riding forced her to take her mind off business, giving her something else to concentrate on.

Today, she continues her association with CNN, but she officially retired in 2001 after discovering the joys of touring and speaking to promote her book, *Play Like a Man, Win Like a Woman.* This book has been translated into twenty-one languages. "I reinvented myself," Gail says. "I don't do things I don't love."

Her second book, *She Wins, You Win,* encourages women to play on the same team in the corporate world. Women are responsible for their own lives, she says, but must support each other to make things work. Too many women are afraid to speak their dreams. "The battle for women to have choices has been fought, but women need to know they have to make decisions," Gail says. "Half of getting something is speaking it and then doing it. Hope is the most unempowering word in the English language because it has nothing to do with action."

Gail has always been self-confident, though she realized as a young child that she would never live up to the world's definition of beauty. So she has never competed in terms of beauty on any level.

"I took beauty out of the equation and just did what needed to be done," Gail says. "I live an intentional life. I never want to be left feeling I would have, could have, or should have."

Freedom to Choose

CAMELIA ADES is an only child.

That was her mother's choice, a remarkable fact considering the conditions in Romania that Camelia was born under. At the time, the country was under the tight rule of Nicolae Ceaucescu, a Communist dictator who firmly controlled the distribution of life's most basic necessities, forbade birth control or family planning, and threatened prison or death to those who performed or received abortions. Despite government encouragement of large families, provisions for children barely covered food or diapers for the first few months of life. Women, who were generally regarded as second-class citizens and treated like animals, were left to fend for themselves, child after child. Many resorted to homemade solutions, such as kitchen chemicals or diaphragm-like devices, to prevent or terminate pregnancies. When Camelia was a teenager her cousin died from an unsafe abortion, leaving two children behind. "I can't tell you how hard it was on me," Camelia says. "I saw firsthand what happened to many women because of the lack of safe medical practices. It took a huge toll on society and the country as a whole."

The story of Camelia's own birth is barbaric. Her mother was forced to endure a Caesarean section without anesthesia, and passed out several times from the pain. Camelia is amazed that her mother survived.

Under the Ceaucescu government, each citizen was allowed only one piece of bread per week, and electricity was strictly rationed. Camelia did her homework by candlelight, wearing gloves to ward off the cold. She garnered hope from reading books and from eavesdropping as her father secretly listened to the "Voice of America" on short-wave radio. "I grew up not trusting men or the government because of what I saw and how women were treated, but with the hope that there was more out there," Camelia says. "It was up to me to discover it. Knowledge is power." The horrors of her youth fueled a passion that drove her to teach herself English and to hope for a better future.

Ceaucescu was overthrown and killed in 1989. Later, Camelia left Romania on a student visa to attend nursing school in Houston. She holds two Master's degrees in nursing, and will soon graduate from the University of Washington with a Ph.D. in nursing and a specialty in women's health.

"So what if I grew up in an austere, depressing environment? I can use that to be a resource for others," Camelia says. "I have dedicated my life to helping women."

Serenity

SOPHIE CANUEL was worried about becoming a new mother. That is, until the moment came.

"All fear fell away the minute I got pregnant," Sophie says. "Suddenly, I knew what to do."

That confidence shows in her peaceful, serene smile as she describes the type of mother she hopes to be. She will tell her children to follow their hearts and will encourage them to follow their dreams, whatever those may be. When a relative questioned Sophie's decision, as a white woman, to have a child with her black husband, Sophie was surprised that such sentiments still existed. But she is not concerned about problems her biracial children may face; kids are taunted for many reasons. "I just want my children to be proud of themselves," Sophie says, "to be accomplished and respected for what they do."

Sophie is a sales representative for a printing company; she also enjoys singing professionally, and is certain her children will be artistic and musical as well. She admires all people who strive to make better lives for themselves, because anything that is changing is growing and growing is beautiful—whether it is flowers, children, or adults changing for the better. Perhaps this knowledge is why Sophie is so much at peace with the life growing inside her, secure in the knowledge that she will one day be proud of how she has raised her baby, "Blues" if it is a girl, or "Sunny" if it is a boy. She won't know which until the moment arrives, but she does know her child will be loved.

Sophie attributes her peaceful state to the loving environment she lives in. She is surrounded by happy people and blessed with a great life, filled with time for introspection. Sophie feels love is the most important thing in the world, because it brings happiness, and that creates beauty.

"When you are happy, your beauty shows," says Sophie. "You have to know yourself and be true to yourself. It is easy to say, but not always easy to do."

Integrity

SHARRON RAGAN turned down the opportunity to compete for Miss Tennessee because she would have had to falsify her image.

"When you are in integrity you are congruent with who you are," Sharron says. "That is beauty."

Sharron had won the title "Miss Carson-Newman" and was ready to represent the Baptist college at the state level. She had entered the local contest completely as herself, rejecting the common "tricks of the trade," and didn't even fix her hair. She had told her parents not to attend the competition because she was sure she wouldn't win. But Sharron did win, and with the crown came advice from a coach on how to compete in the Miss Tennessee contest—change her focus in the talent contest, reshape her eyebrows, and invest in a new dress. Sharron rejected the idea and stepped down as Miss Carson-Newman. "To get to the next level, I would have had to be someone different, something fake," Sharron says. She has never regretted her decision. "I felt like I would have had to be untrue to who I was."

Sharron calls herself an "Intuitive." Her business, BIOS (Brand, Insight, Opportunity and Strategy) helps senior leaders of major corporations define their visual and verbal identities, using their inner thoughts to discover who they are. Sharron intentionally developed her own intuition after frequently experiencing strong thoughts about people she did not know, especially in large crowds. She has translated that skill into helping people utilize the energy around them to define their careers and move their businesses forward. "There was always something within me that made me feel different. I could feel it and I acted on it," she says. "My goal is to help as many people as possible find their integrity."

Born in Mobile, Alabama, Sharron grew up in a small town near Charleston, Tennessee, on a river in the woods. People often told her she was a beautiful child, but those words of praise didn't mean much to Sharron, who didn't think outer beauty was important. "I wanted people to see how I was on the inside," Sharron says. "True beauty is being in a place where you are at peace. It's all about who you are."

Sharron may have turned down the opportunity to compete for a beauty title, but she won a greater prize: integrity.

Reciprocity

CLEA KORE carries on a tradition of helping young students because she benefited from similar help years ago.

Clea was a young woman when she left the tiny apartment in Germany where her Polish parents had settled after the horrors of World War II. (Her father had spent a year in an American prisoner-of-war camp, and her mother had seen people walking from Dresden with their skin peeling away from the effects of bombing.) Clea traveled from Geneva to Rome, working as an au pair and as a model, gaining a love of language, literature, and travel. But it wasn't until after her daughter was born that Clea considered pursuing a formal education. Having a baby hadn't been a happy experience. Her friends had rejected her, as had the baby's father, who stated he needed a child "like a hole in the head." Clea says those were anxious and depressing years. "I went into a deep, blue space. I had never valued my life," Clea says. "Then I realized I needed to become somebody, for my daughter."

She contacted a family she had worked for and asked for a loan so she could go to school. They were more generous than she had dreamed, paying her tuition at South Connecticut State College and inviting her and her daughter to live in their basement apartment in New Haven. They told her they were merely "continuing the legacy" of a good deed the woman had benefited from years earlier, when a similar act of generosity allowed her to go to college, with only one condition: that she help someone else one day. "They changed my life," Clea says. "To this day I am grateful to them."

Clea flourished in the academic world. She received a scholarship to Yale the first year women were accepted, and graduated summa cum laude. Next came graduate school at Stanford, with a Danforth Fellowship. Today Clea is an adjunct professor at Cabrillo Community College in California, and a lecturer at California State, Monterrey Bay. She often pays tuition for students or gives someone a place to stay, passing on the tradition she learned from her own benefactor, and encourages the students to carry on the practice when the opportunity comes. "I am so fortunate to be able to help them," Clea says.

Now happily married, she is also thankful for her husband and daughter, and for her spiritual journey and Buddhist philosophy. Mostly, she is thankful that she is no longer the tragic person she used to be. "I'm very happy with what I've become."

Perseverance

HELENE HINES does not know the meaning of "give up."

At the age of thirty, she was diagnosed with multiple sclerosis. Her answer to this crippling disease was to continue her active lifestyle. In fact, she began to run in marathons, and completed twenty-seven before her muscle degeneration became severe enough to necessitate the use of a wheelchair. The last marathon Helene ran on foot was in 1999; shortly after, she began to experience numbness in her legs and spasms of the esophagus that made it difficult to breathe. Even then, she continued to compete in marathons, using a push-rim wheelchair. When her vertigo worsened so she could no longer lean forward in the chair, she switched to a hand cycle, a recumbent-style bicycle that she rides by turning the wheels with her hands. Helene continues to log winning times whenever she competes, despite the increasing physical challenges. Helene could not train at her regular level for the 2005 New York City Marathon because of nerve pain in her back, but she nonetheless completed the race in one hour and forty-five minutes, just three minutes shy of her best time using the cycle.

Helene is an active member of Long Island Achilles Club, an athletic club for people with disabilities. She works to ensure all athletes get the recognition they deserve, and teaches water aerobics classes for others with MS. She also trains people with various disabilities for competition in races. "Everyone I train does well," Helene says. "I tell them to place their mind on their objectives and let their bodies follow."

A recent diagnosis of kidney cancer forced Helene to stop the electro stimulation muscle treatment which she believes reduces the devastating effects of MS. Despite this additional challenge, she continues to train for marathons and to fight for the cause she is passionate about. Helene is currently in remission from the cancer but admits it has decreased the intensity of her training schedule. However, a newfound passion, painting, now has a priority in her life. "I found this new thing that I love," Helene says, with the positive and energetic spirit that helps her keep a fast pace, in life as well as in competition.

Dr. George Hines, her husband of thirty-five years, uses two words to describe Helene: enthusiasm and determination. He says she is the toughest person he has ever met, but Helene plays down the compliment.

"It's just saying 'I'm going to finish it' and putting one foot in front of the other."

song for Johanna

ADELE GRAF

song for Johanna

for my grandmother, Johanna

your Yiddish exuberance
slowed my young, friskey legs
along our wooded path,
your *Oy vi sheyns* pronouncing pleasure
in these trees far from
your asphalt urban home

oh how lovely you were too!
your speaking voice a lilt, sparkling in song,
grandmother now myself,
I too sing the songs you knew,
wrap my tongue around their foreign
yet familiar sounds

in *"Sheyn vi di Levoneh"* my voice rises
from the choir, shining through –
lovely as the moon, your radiance
still waxes, never wanes,
beaming into twinkling skies,
brightening dim nights

now I sing with you, Johanna,
now I sing for you

The Road Near Two Gray Hills

DAVID FEELA

A Navajo woman knows how to weave a rug
as if it were as natural as breathing.
She plucks at the warp like a grandmother
picking lint from an old sweater
but the pattern climbs like a beautiful moss
up the north side of her loom so slowly
the children think she does nothing all day long.
The sun comes up, the sun goes down
And nothing between but the rhythm
caught fast in the tangle of weft.
At night she unbraids her children's hair
And combs it smooth, telling stories
of the old ways when animals spoke in riddles
to guard their secrets from those
who would unravel the world for themselves.
If she finally closes her eyes
it is only to better hear her children breathing
amid the shuttle of light on the highway
and the bleating of sheep in the field.

Native American Beauty

RUBY CONE has learned the true definition of beauty the hard way.

As a young girl, she did everything she could to fit into the American ideal, even developing what she now realizes was an eating disorder. Now, when she looks at photos of herself as a teenager, the thin, drawn face that looks back shocks her. "I thought I looked great, but I was really sick," Ruby says. She had always felt pressure to lose weight in order to fit in, even from her relatives on the nearby Navajo reservation. "I thought it was strange. Where did they get that from?" Ruby now believes television and movies helped create an unrealistic ideal of beauty. She has come to reject that ideal and to recognize beauty in women who radiate joy and confidence through their smiles and countenances. "I see a purity of heart, an inner peace," Ruby says. "It is nice to be around someone who has self-assurance."

For herself, he has adopted a new, healthier ideal of beauty based on joy and confidence. She smiles when she thinks about how her life has changed. Ruby and her husband David recently renewed their wedding vows as a commitment of love to one another. They work together, selling ukuleles to people all over the world. Ironically, Ruby long dreamed of playing the flute in an orchestra, but she loves her job and is very thankful for her life. Her dream is to get to the end of a long life knowing that she has done her best to serve God.

There is one message she intends to pass on to the children she hopes to have. "I know what the American stereotype can do to people. I hope that if I have a daughter or even a son, I can show them what true beauty is," Ruby says. "Man's view of beauty is not important. What is more important is what God thinks of you."

Ruby knows it will be difficult to instill her own definition of beauty in her children because of images on television and what they will learn from their peers. Despite still being exposed to those same images and ideals, she finally considers herself to be beautiful, just as she is.

"God made me who I am," Ruby says. "He formed me—how could I not like that?"

Tropical Beauty

BETH DIEHL fled Cuba with her family when she was a young girl.

They took only what they could fit into a suitcase, certain they would return as soon as Castro was defeated. Beth didn't mind sharing a one-bedroom apartment in Miami with her mother, father, four of her five brothers, and two cousins, because she knew their large home, spacious yard, and servants were waiting back in her homeland.

Castro's unexpected success closed the doors to return, and Miami became their new home. Beth only recently returned to Cuba, after more than forty years. Tears come to her eyes as she talks of her long-awaited return to her childhood home. The tropical beauty she remembered had been replaced with poverty and scarcity.

Beth's life has been filled with extremes. She was born into a wealthy Cuban family that suffered unexpected hardships. Her first husband died from alcohol-related complications at a young age. She and her current husband, Rick, have built a successful business during a quarter century of marriage. They enjoy spending time with their four daughters and four granddaughters at their spacious waterfront home, which is surrounded by palm trees and reminiscent of her homeland.

Ironically, Beth's favorite memories are of her childhood in that tiny Miami apartment, playing in the street with cousins and newfound friends. Surrounded with family, Beth was comforted by a strong faith and hope for better things to come, despite the hardships. Her mother adjusted to the sudden change of fortune and the worries about relatives who had stayed behind (especially Beth's fifth brother, who was put into prison for resisting the new regime), and learned to cook and care for the extended family.

Beth experienced prejudice as a young Cuban girl in the United States. Adjusting to life in Miami, she was frequently "labeled" by her name and heritage, and she struggled with classes taught in English, which she did not speak. The prejudice continued after her family moved to San Antonio; her school friends would lie to their parents about their friendship with a Hispanic girl. Even today, Beth feels some people are afraid to get too close to her because of the riches her family is blessed with. She says prejudice comes from every angle and the desire to not be different is present in every culture. Although the Latino culture values physical beauty, Beth learned to value inner beauty from her mother, who was humble despite her privileged upbringing. Beth knows the true riches her family is blessed with.

"When a woman has a true relationship with Christ that flows through her and shows in how she relates to her family," Beth says, "that makes her beautiful."

Warmth

ALEKSANDRA VANDER-HOEK caught the last plane out of Poland before martial law was implemented.

She was twenty-eight years old and had answered a plea from her uncle in Montreal who needed assistance with his mentally handicapped daughter. Aleksandra never returned to her homeland, leaving her family behind. Efforts to communicate with them were blocked or censored. Aleksandra applied for a temporary visa at the Canadian Consulate, but she was quietly advised to apply for a longer term.

She settled in Calgary and now shares a fulfilling life with her Dutch–Canadian husband, who proposed when she cried while watching the movie "Sophie's Choice,' their son and two daughters. Raising her children in a different culture with no support from family was a struggle that taught Aleksandra awareness and tolerance of others.

"It was an incredible challenge, but also rewarding," Aleksandra says, adding she still struggles with issues regarding her autistic son's education. "He can be a terror or a godsend, but he is the best thing in my life."

Aleksandra greets strangers as if they were old friends, with warm hugs and genuine hellos. Her passion for living is equally evident in other areas of her life. She is an accomplished professional pianist and a math teacher and also has a master's degree in economics. She speaks English, Polish, and Russian fluently.

"As a professional, a mother, a partner, and a lover, I communicate in English," Aleksandra says, noting she has now lived in Canada longer than in Poland. "I still pray in Polish."

Aleksandra has always valued education over beauty. When she was a teenager in Poland, her heroes were women poets and explorers, not the movie stars other girls admired. She says she was a little mischievous and at times her sense of humor would get her into trouble with the teachers. What appeared to some as a lack of respect was really Aleksandra's belief that no one person is more important than any other. She joyfully remembers the time Pope John Paul II danced with her and a group of young adults she had taken on a tour to the Castle Gandolfo.

"If the Queen came to my front door, I would invite her in to tea," Aleksandra says, with an ease that eluded her while she was growing up. "I was ugly and skinny as a teenager, a late bloomer. Now I have a lot of self-confidence."

Fast Talent

GWEN FAYE recently gave something up in order to discover a latent talent that had been trying to break through the surface of her identity all her life.

"I gave up TV for forty days, and it changed my whole life," Gwen says.

During her fast from television, Gwen began to write poetry. By the end of the first week she had written enough to fill a book she had created with handmade paper. Friends encouraged her to publish more copies of that book, *The Fine Art of Caring.*

Gwen now shares her poetry with others at Crochet Cafés—classes, held at local cafés, that combine crocheting lessons and poetry readings. Gwen is also gathering a following of other crochet and art lovers into the Crochet Nation, a "nation" complete with a national anthem and the motto, "One Nation under Yarn." Gwen credits God with leading her to Atlanta, where friends have encouraged her to discover who she is and share her talents with the world. "Tapping into who I am has opened doors for me," Gwen says. "Crochet Café allows me to do all the things I love: ministry, poetry, music, business, art, and design."

Gwen believes she has an unusual balance between the right and left sides of her brain, allowing her to combine artistic talents with organizational and entrepreneurial skills. As a young girl she loved to create model communities using common materials such as construction paper and matchsticks, despite a lack of encouragement from her family in artistic and creative endeavors. She also participated regularly in such school activities as cheerleading, track, music, and student council, even though her family often moved due to her father's military career. She was self-confident, positive, and popular but there was something else she dreamed of becoming: an artist. Giving up television helped Gwen discover a wealth of inner talent that has defined her newfound passion for creativity.

"My heart's desire is to inspire others and help them find the childhood dreams they forgot about when they became adults," Gwen says, adding that her greatest accomplishment is becoming herself. "I'm the best I've ever been."

Gwen Faye

Imperfect Beauty

Danielle Ackley-McPhail

No pale, pastel princess —
I am a dark and lively earth-mother
    cloaked in deep, rich hues,
    my life displayed upon my face.

No perfect coiffure of crowning ringlets —
My tresses are wild and loose
    free to catch the wind and sun,
    tangled by the essence of my living.

No veiled social gaze —
Look into my eyes and reflect
    that the common woman
    is anything but common.

No pure gold heart —
Mine is of mere flesh
    capable of hate,
    though love is easier.

No graceful arms with dainty, folded hands
Mine are open wide,
    willing to embrace the world
    and reach for dreams.

No waif-like frame —
I have the width of hip
    to populate a nation,
    and the wisdom to wait.

No proper, mincing steps —
My strides are wide
    devouring the distance
    between me and my goal.

Not alone —
I am a world of people.
    We are what is real
    in a world of false images.

I am not, I am

SHIRLEY A. JONES

I am not a poet.
But, I have
happiness, sadness,
imagination, and thoughts.
I have fantasies,
I am a dreamer.

I am not a political activist.
But, I have
dreams, aspirations,
goals, and ideas.
I have hope.
I am a visionary.

I am not a pillar of the community.
But, I have
strength, convictions,
opinions, and spirit.
I have emotion.
I am a sentimentalist.

I am a dreamer,
a visionary,
a sentimentalist.
Let me dream.
Let me hope.
Let me feel.
Let me be impractical.

Delayed Dreams

IRIS GRIMM grew up knowing her choices were very limited.

Growing up in communist East Germany, she held fast to two seemingly impossible dreams: to see the Grand Canyon and to work in another country. The government kept a close watch on her family because her parents were well-educated and had relatives in West Germany. Iris was rejected for admission to a sports school at age fourteen because officials feared she would find an opportunity to defect. She was almost denied acceptance into a boarding school as well, because students from farming families and the children of physical laborers were given priority under the communist system. Iris faced similar roadblocks in college. A university professor told her that to be accepted into the tourism program, she must take advanced Russian, join the Communist Party, and cut all ties with her West German relatives.

Torn between her dreams and the ideals of others, Iris sought her father's advice. He told her the choice was hers, but that at the end of the day, she should like what she saw when she looked in the mirror. Iris chose to reject the university's demands and study economics, but continued to wonder what might have happened had she conceded. She had every reason to expect she would spend her life working at a government-assigned job, with no chance for other opportunities.

Then on November 9, 1989, while riding the bus to school, she noticed a man with a grin on his face.

"I skipped work and went to West Berlin," he told her. "I walked through the wall."

Iris and the other students had heard nothing of the Berlin Wall's coming down; there had been no official announcement. She immediately went to West Germany with her father to visit their relatives. A world of opportunities became available to Iris, and she took advantage of the newfound freedom, not knowing what the changing future held. "Sometimes it is better not to know," she says. "If you have a dream, you have to just do it."

One of the first things she did when she came to the United States was to visit the Grand Canyon. Iris now lives in Atlanta with her husband and two dogs, and works as a "Success Advocate," providing stress and time-management counseling to physicians and health care workers. Thanks to the coming of freedom to East Germany, the impossible dreams of her childhood have come true.

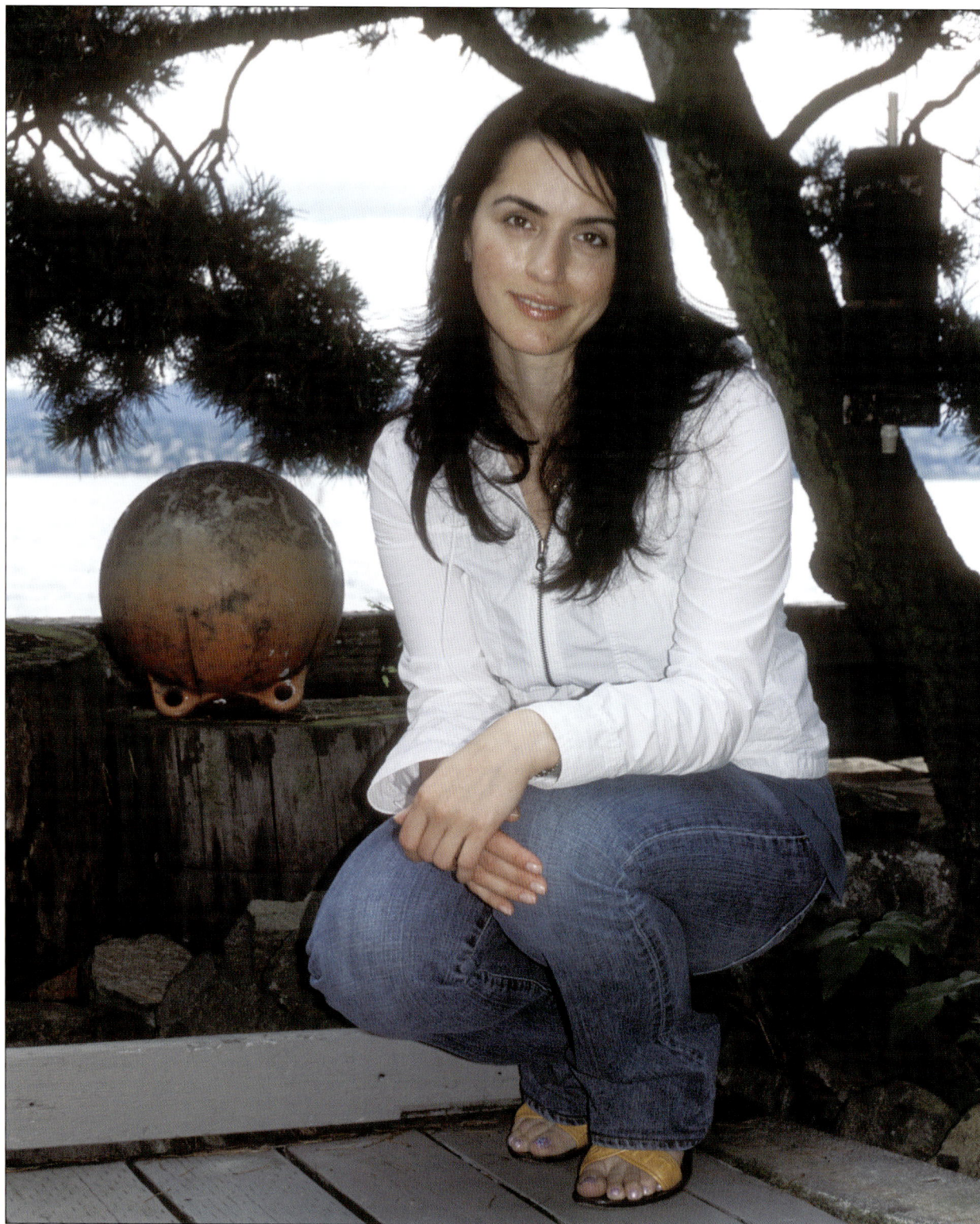

International Scholar

CAMELIA ESPAHBOD looks back on the years after she left her husband as the hardest time of her life—even worse than her childhood in Tehran, when her family spent many nights in an underground shelter while the sirens of war sounded.

"It wasn't good," Camelia says. "We would wonder if a bomb would drop on our heads." The memory of one tragic night, when a family friend's engagement party was cut short by a bomb that killed thirty people, remains fresh in her mind.

After finishing high school, Camelia left Iran to study abroad. She taught herself enough Russian to pass an entrance exam so she could enter dental school in Kiev at the age of nineteen. "I was so focused on that," Camelia says. "I was always in the library, the first one to get there and the last one to leave."

After some time working as a dentist in Kiev, she moved back to Tehran and married an Iranian-born American citizen, assuming he would have an open mind. Instead, he proved abusive, and soon after they moved to California she realized she wanted out of the marriage. Unable to speak English, she had difficulty dealing with lawyers as she struggled to obtain a green card and to begin divorce proceedings. She had few friends, and only her mother offered support from home. Even other women in abusive marriages urged her to give her husband another chance. Camelia now tells women not to be naïve about marriage and relationships. "If there is physical or emotional abuse, there is no respect," she advises. "If you are having a hard time, if you are not happy with your life, don't feel sorry for yourself. Do something and stand up for yourself, no matter what."

After her divorce, Camelia was once again faced with learning a new language in order to open the door to education, this time in English. She received her American dental license in August of 2004, and is currently enrolled in a master's degree program at the University of Washington. She works with two other dentists, one of whom treats primarily Russian-speaking patients.

Camelia has worked very hard to get where she is today. She now shares a beautiful waterfront home with her boyfriend, and enjoys painting and training for triathlons.

"I am most proud of my accomplishments, being able to leave bad things behind, making my life better and better, standing up for myself," Camelia says. "For a while I had a hard time talking about the past, but I am very happy now."

Soul Music

NATHALIE GEDDRY admits that the first time she performed in public was a challenge. "It was hard to put my music out there," she says. "That is my soul, my words."

Nathalie's natural creative ability took a detour when she was in high school. Her family had moved to Fredericton, New Brunswick, a small town where it was difficult to make new friends. "I would have started singing publicly a lot sooner if not for the Fredericton experience," she says. "It took a lot of years to peel that away and for the real me to come out."

Nathalie went on to college and obtained a degree in translation, but an economic recession made it difficult for her to find a job in that field. So she took an entrepreneurial leap and started her own translation business with the help of a government loan that was interest-free for one year. That first year was a struggle, but Nathalie managed to pay off the entire loan on the very last day. "I was very poor, but I paid it off," she says. "That was my goal."

Her translation business, now in its eleventh year, supports her pursuit of fame in the music industry. Nathalie's recording career got an unexpected boost in 2002, when a friend challenged her to enter a singing competition of French contemporary music. Encouraged by winning second place, Nathalie entered again the following year and won the title. She subsequently received a grant to record a compact disc. "Liberté," the title song, was number one on the Maritimes music charts for six weeks.

"Approche-toi," also written and performed by Nathalie, is now climbing the charts throughout Canada. As she bares her soul through her music, she is learning a life lesson: to finally like the person she has become, without worrying about what others think.

Nathalie and her husband live in a modest home that overlooks the Atlantic Ocean near Halifax, Nova Scotia. She spends much of her free time composing and performing with her band, working hard to sell records at gigs and from her Web site, www.nathaliegeddry.com. She says her dream to be an "overnight success" is worth the hard work.

"Living off my music. That is what I wish for when I blow out my candles."

Balance

ALLISON HUSBAND has, by her own account, achieved a sense of balance most of us only dream of.

In her life, no one thing overpowers the importance of any other. Home, work, family and even a satisfying relationship with her ex-husband seem to flow effortlessly in the midst of Allison's active lifestyle. She refuses to let life get the best of her, often making difficult choices to maintain the balance. She sticks to what she believes in and devotes all her energy and time to things she deems important, such as taking an extra hour to jog the long way home from work or spending her vacation time volunteering as the head nurse at a diabetes camp. Her sense of adventure took her to Australia for two years to add experience to her master's degree in nursing.

Allison is not afraid to be unconventional, if that is what it takes to maintain harmony. When it became apparent that she and her husband had grown apart and "out of love," they made the decision to separate and to keep their children's needs above their own. He now lives down the street and continues to take equal responsibility for their son and daughter. Allison says it is the perfect arrangement for them. They respect each other and although they are both involved in long-term relationships, they feel divorce is unnecessary. "We are both very happy now," Allison says. "Our children haven't suffered at all."

It takes effort to create balance in one's life, but Allison grew up observing the benefits of healthy living. Her dad walked miles to and from work, regardless of the weather, and she credits him with giving her the love of an active lifestyle. She is an avid downhill skier, and her vacations often include long bicycle tours. She regularly takes time for herself by biking or jogging to work, ignoring the pressures of our "hurry up" world. It pays great dividends.

"I'm full of energy," she says. For Allison that energy translates into happiness, health, and true beauty.

ANJA LEIGH

The first time
I read my poetry out loud
    I cried.
    I did.
So stunned
by the sound of my voice
running through the range
of raw emotion
    I cried.
    I did.
My voice was fallow as fields
where ancestral babushka women
birthed their silent dreams
waiting to be heard.
Now I was the voice
of their thoughts and hopes.
But I was a
young willow woman
bending to every breeze
still writing the pages of my life.
    I stopped writing my poetry
    and walked away.
Quietly, the women behind me
stood on each other's shoulders
reaching up to break
the long line of silence.
They handed me buckets of words
and blankets of verse:
    Speak up.
    Speak out.

One day
I read my poetry out loud.
My voice was fearless, full of
mothers and grandmothers,
sisters, aunts, and daughters.
And all those women behind me
waiting for a voice,
wept for joy.

Prayer for a Day

JILL WILLIAMS

Please let's not bitch about hairs turning gray.
Or dwell on the years we want back.
Instead let's dance gladly with Spirit today.

On journeys of joy in a magical sleigh,
Past mirrors that don't ever crack.
Please! Let's not bitch about hairs turning gray.

Or fret when our eyelids begin to decay
And puff up like spuds in a sack.
Instead let's dance gladly with Spirit today.

Enjoy April sunlight, each welcoming ray.
There's always a picnic to pack!
Let us not bitch about hairs turning gray,

Or how the news headlines are never okay,
And futures are fading to black.
Instead let's dance gladly with Spirit today.

Be happy. Be thankful. Be open to pray.
Real gratitude keeps us on track.
I will not moan about hairs turning gray.
Instead I'll dance gladly with Spirit today.

Commitment

MAILE ROUNDTREE has been married seven times—to her husband of seven years.

They renew their vows every year to take a pulse on their marriage. This year they hired a coach to help them plan a forty-day sabbatical from their relationship. They had no communication with each other and put all major decisions on hold during that time. The experience gave them a new sense of commitment. "After forty days I realized that he was always going to choose me," Maile says, adding that the ultimate decision would always be up to her. "We've both chosen to be one hundred percent responsible for our marriage, in generosity and in play."

Maile, a third generation Fijian, grew up traveling the world first class with her father, who worked for American Airlines. She meant to continue traveling as an adult, working odd jobs between extended trips, but love had other plans. She met her husband while taking a Landmark Education course in Seattle. That course also gave her another gift—the strength to deal with two episodes of sexual abuse from her childhood, one by an elderly male family friend and another by a female babysitter who also abused her younger brother. Those experiences affected Maile deeply. "I did have a lot of low self-esteem issues. I would date men who reflected that," she says. "I didn't think I deserved any better."

Maile said the Landmark Education course enabled her to stop "filling in the blanks" with unrealistic memories. She regained power and developed the self-confidence to start her own business as an event planner and wedding coordinator. Today, she owns "Vintage Vixen," a line of handmade jewelry that is sold in stores all over the world. Maile is firmly rooted to life in the Seattle suburbs, but she takes every opportunity to travel. She loves to discover the new geography, people, art, and food of an unfamiliar city.

Maile survived a battle with cervical cancer several years ago. She has fully recovered, but since her mother had taken DES before she was born and "DES daughters" often have difficulty conceiving, Maile until recently planned not to have children. Now, she is re-thinking that decision.

"What do I want my life to be about? Life is about growing," Maile says. "You can have your dreams: just take the first step and start living your dreams instead of hoping for 'someday.'"

Explorer

YOLANTA SZULE was willing to do whatever it took to better her life—including leaving her family and everything she owned behind to come to a new continent in search of work.

When Yolanta was twenty-nine, she boarded a New York-bound plane in her native Poland, hoping to find better job opportunities abroad, even though she had no plans and no one to meet her in the United States. She says she was lucky from the beginning; she could have been denied permission to leave at all. Luck stayed with her on the plane. She met a woman from Poland who lived in New York, and Yolanta had a temporary place to stay before they even landed. But she knew only one word in English: "Hi."

It wasn't long before she got a job and started her new life working her way from one job to another, learning a new language and culture. Yolanta soon had a manicurist license, and today she enjoys her work at a salon in Manhattan, where she easily jokes with her customers in English, Polish, and Russian. Her outgoing nature helped her make friends, who showed her around town. Yolanta learned English along the way, but it wasn't easy. "It was hard to come here. I would pretend I was okay, but I really wasn't," she says. "I am proud of the fact that I traveled to this new world on my own, got a job, and learned new skills and a new language."

She had learned her sense of style from her mother, who always made sure Yolanta and her identical twin sister looked perfect in every detail. Yolanta admits she still dresses to impress her mother, but she now has a more relaxed view of beauty. "I think a woman who is natural, casual, and clean is beautiful. I feel beautiful, happy, and relaxed when I spend time in the woods, or go driving in the country with my boyfriend, but I am always ready to come back to New York City," Yolanta says. "It's exciting."

Yolanta has now lived in New York for fifteen years; she became a U. S. citizen three years ago. The spirit of exploration remains, though. She travels around the United States, to Puerto Rico, and back to Poland when she can.

Her fearless spirit allowed Yolanta to leap into an unknown world in search of a better life, and she has never regretted it.

Conqueror

DEVON WEBSTER is the picture of health.

Short, cropped hair frames her rosy, pixie-like face and her bright, smiling eyes. Her svelte frame reflects the many sporting events she competes in—despite ongoing physical struggles. Multiple Sclerosis landed her in intensive care when she was a teen and left her barely able to move for months. When she returned to high school two years later, she was bald, in a wheelchair, academically behind her classmates, and faced with rejection. "The boys in the hall would bark at me and call me a dog," she says, adding she chose to be strengthened by the ordeal. "It made me defiant. I felt above it. The whole experience strengthened my sense of self."

It was very hard for her parents—who had adopted Devon when she was an infant—to later send her off to college, knowing she would have to fend for herself. Devon says she regained her strength while living alone as she pushed her weakened body beyond its supposed limitations. Intense physical therapy, experimental chemotherapy, and sheer determination helped the process. "I basically did all the things I was told not to do," Devon says. "I was in college and on my own, and I just took control of things."

Her health remains her biggest struggle because she never knows when her body may lose the strength she has worked so hard for. A recent bout with breast cancer helped her choose the disease as a specialty in her oncology fellowship, which she will soon complete at the University of Washington (she is already board certified in internal medicine). Devon opted for a single mastectomy and radiation to battle the cancer, in part because she had dealt with mortality issues at an early age. Her ex-girlfriend gave her an unusual gift after the mastectomy. She had a star in the constellation of Leo, Devon's sign, named "Weez," the same name she had bestowed on Devon's now-gone right breast. On the anniversary of the mastectomy Devon holds a Weez party, complete with breast-shaped food, as a memorial but also as a celebration of her continuing and optimistic life.

When Devon recently met her birth mother she was surprised to recognize features similar to her own, because she had never looked like anyone else. Her own definition of a beautiful woman is one who embodies a spirit that says, "I get to take up space in the world," with a healthy dose of humor.

"If you are not constantly amused by life, you are not paying attention," Devon says. "Everything makes me laugh."

Born in Canada, Linda learned to speak English as a teenager after moving to Labrador City, NL. She worked several years as a flight attendant for a major airline. She married and moved to Texas, where her twin daughters were born. Widowed, Linda remarried and decided to further her education. A fond memory is when the girls joined her at the kitchen table to do homework while she was doing her own algebra assignments. Linda obtained a B. A. in Applied Design and Visual Arts and in Communication from the University of Houston-Clear Lake. She started Lapointe Documentary Photography shortly after. She currently lives in the Houston area with husband Drew and serves as a Stephen minister at her church.

Linda's work has been published in newspapers, in art and literary magazines, and in the 2006 Bay Area Houston Economic Development coffee-table book. She has photographed the work of missionaries in Ethiopia, India, Mexico, Panama, and on Navajo reservations. A photograph taken in India appears on the United Nations' 2005 World Summit website. Exhibited photos taken on a National Geographic photography expedition to Bhutan have won awards two years in a row. In May of 2002, Linda was honored for her service to the art community.

Patty Mayeux

Patty was born in a suburb of Cleveland, OH and moved to New Orleans when she was fifteen. She graduated from Tulane University and moved to Lake Charles, LA shortly after marrying her husband, Steve. They live on the bay in Galveston, TX. Their two daughters currently live in Dallas, TX. While they were young, Patty worked at many varied part-time jobs, including teaching special education and preschool, developing and overseeing her church youth program, and serving in volunteer capacities as girl scout leader, PTA officer and civic leader, to name a few. Her writing career includes news and magazine features, in print as well as online.

Patty enjoys traveling, reading, speaking, writing, art, music and volunteering for various organizations. She delivers personal development coaching through ELAN (Elevating Life Attitudes Now) Enterprises, of which she is the sole owner. She has received various awards and recognitions throughout her professional, educational and volunteer career, but the accomplishment that she is most proud of is the one she has worked the hardest at: her two grown daughters. Patty admits that the real credit goes to them and to God for leading them both to a joy-filled life following his plan and serving others. They are both the most beautiful women she knows.

To order more copies of
Beautiful Women – Like You and Me

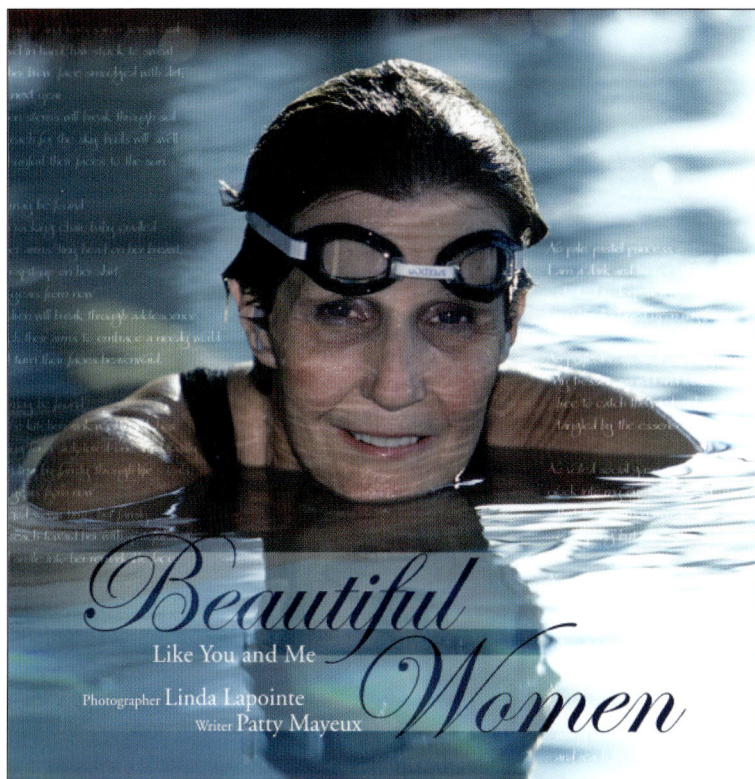

This book makes a great gift for mothers, sisters, and friends.

It is a necessary addition for women's studies departments of educational institutions, as the theme addresses the concern that our society discourages women by pushing an unrealistic ideal of physical perfection.

Beautiful Women – Like You and Me can be read in short episodes, making it a wonderful supplement to any doctor's office or waiting room.

For more information or to order copies go to:
www.bwbooks.net

Or write to: BW Books
2437 Bay Area Boulevard, # 149
Houston, TX 77058

Or email: info@bwbooks.net

Or call: (281) 728-7618